Spirituality in Counseling

A Clinician's Guide to Incorporate the
Spiritual Competencies Endorsed
by the American Counseling Association

by Dr. Sharon H. Harrell, LPCMH

PITTSBURGH, PENNSYLVANIA 15222

RoseDog Books
701 Smithfield Street
Pittsburgh, PA 15222
Visit our website at *www.rosedogbookstore.com*

ISBN: 978-1-4809-1750-7
eISBN: 978-1-4809-1728-6

I have intentionally used different translations of the Scripture for ease of use and clarity: so to illustrate meaning in therapy.

DEDICATION

This book is dedicated to the reader: clinicians, clients, students, and other partakers who have an interest with spirituality in counseling.

In Memory of my Father
James Calvin Harwell

Zechariah 4:6
New International Version (NIV)
6 So he said to me, "This is the word of the LORD to Zerubbabel: 'Not by might nor by power, but by my Spirit,' says the LORD Almighty.

ACKNOWLEDGMENTS

To God be the Glory for What he has done. I am so grateful and thankful for my journey, where God has taken me as he continues to lead and guide me. This is the LORD'S doing, and words of gratitude are boundless; I have felt your presence and your grace. Praise the Lord!

To my Mom: Evon Lewis Harwell for your gracious support and love through everything, you kept the faith in me and for continual prayers that sustain me. I am so proud to be your daughter.

To my Children: Douglass and Tyler words cannot convey my love and appreciation for you both. Being your mom is my greatest joy and privilege.

To my sister: Sandra Monroe you have encouraged me all the while, thanks for your belief in me.

To my cherished granddaughter: Ja'lyah Marie, I am a nana now.

To my Christian church family and Pastor Kenneth E. Gaines at Spirit Life Ministries, International: your prayers and embolden helped me to strive toward my goal with "pressing to new levels and finishing strong".

To American Institute of Holistic Theology: the opportunity to pursue my academic dream with the degree completion Doctor of Holistic Theology, ThD. I am elated to have attained such an inspirational education within a holistic milieu that is interfaith and integrated for the study of religion and spirituality. It was an amazing and affirming experience for me.

Special thanks to my friends: who have influenced, motivated, and inspired me, which made an impact through-out this process. I hold in admiration the divine connections that helped thrust me towards my aspiration.

To my colleagues in the mental health field: my heartfelt thanks for your faithful dedication and professionalism that enriched my growth and development as counselor.

To Mark Coffey, thank you for your insightful review of my work, when I was baffled, helped me gain a new perspective.

ABSTRACT

Spirituality in Counseling: a Clinician's Guide to Incorporate the Spiritual Competencies Endorsed by the American Counseling Association (ACA).

Dr. Sharon H. Harrell, LPCMH

The therapeutic process is about the client and warrants careful attention to create methods that resonate with his or her beliefs and frame of reference. The contemporary study of spirituality in counseling encompasses a wide range of theories, therapies, and interests. The Association of Spiritual, Ethical, and Religious Values in Counseling (ASERVIC) and the American Counseling Association (ACA) endorse including spirituality in counseling. Developing clinician's awareness of spirituality is crucial to ethical, multicultural, wellbeing, mental health theory and practice. ASERVIC has developed a list of competencies for helping professionals addressing spiritual and religious issues in counseling, giving practitioners the support to address spirituality in counseling. This dissertation explores each spiritual competency using multiple counseling modalities, recommendations, and intervention approaches for clinicians to incorporate spirituality into counseling that works with real depth, and is authentic and effective in helping the client, while promoting healing, growth, and well-being.

Forward

The major professional organizations have recognized the importance of spirituality in counseling practice with the development of fourteen core spiritual competencies to address spiritual and religious issues in counseling. This dissertation will examine and explore the spiritual competencies as endorsed by the American Counseling Association (ACA) as a guide for clinicians to incorporate spirituality in counseling.

TABLE OF CONTENTS

I.
Introduction and Purpose of Counseling

The aim of counseling is to facilitate the development of the whole person: the integration of mind, body, and spirit (Hinterkopf xxii). Spirituality is identified as a part of the basic human experience, a dimension that surfaces frequently in counseling issues (Hinterkopf 1). Sperry asserts that spirituality is a "vital" aspect of human evolution and elemental for individuals dealing with life problems and finding meaning in life; it requires attention in the counseling process (1). Counseling and spirituality seek a common goal: human healing, growth, and fulfillment. Effective counseling addresses the body, mind, and spirit to promote healing and optimal well-being (Corey 117). Counseling in the twenty-first century has evolved to recognize the role of spirituality and religion in clients' lives (Blando 1). Recently, a holistic view of the counseling has arisen that addresses a client's spiritual life and features the whole person—body, mind, and spirit. This development is considered fundamental to the counseling profession (Cashwell and Young 21, 26): It is the spiritual element that synthesizes the whole person and provides some sense of direction and order.

The purpose of counseling extends to enriching personal development, problem solving, and overcoming emotional and mental stressors; it provide the footing for exploration and inclusion of religious and spiritual factors as well as all psychosocial factors that affect clients' lives (Kelly 42). Richards and Bergin contend that the core principle for counseling/psychotherapy is to improve clients' coping skills and settle their presenting issues and concerns to further promote healing, growth, and wellness. This goal of therapy can

1

be enhanced by integrating spiritual or religious elements to foster human maturation (154). Plante describes the trend provided by contemporary mental health professionals as more about advancing clients' functionality, efficiency, and nourishing lifestyle with strategies and interventions that help to increase their ability to cope with common stressors (27). He affirms that counseling brings to light issues that pertain to meaning, purpose, life choices, way of life, questioning, and life's distasteful situations, such as grief, loss, relational conflicts, and disenchantments. It helps clients manage their lives more constructively, using their strengths and weaknesses to treat the whole person and promote wellness. Incorporating religion/spirituality can offer wisdom and functional guidance when appropriate and desired (Plante 27).

Operational Definitions

For the purpose of this book, the tenets of religion and spirituality are identified as having distinct terminology and meanings. One way to differentiate between spirituality and religion is to view spirituality as a natural form of life, a quality that is inherent in all human beings (Burke and Miranti 12). This requires that spirituality be distinguished from religion with distinctions relevant to the worldviews and philosophical orientations of each client being served. Every culture and society has definitions for the experience of spirituality. Spirituality signifies a unique, personally meaningful experience (Hinterkopf 9). Hinterkopf asserts that a clear definition of spirituality aids the counselor when appropriately addressing the client's spiritual issues whether the client's spirituality is adjoined with a religion or not (9). Spirituality is considered more inclusive than religion (Meier, O'Connor, and Vankatwky 2) and less controversial when understood as a construct of human development that is innate to human beings (Ingersoll 108). Ingersoll describes spirituality as possessing both tangible and intangible elements (100).

The Association for Spiritual, Ethical, and Religious Values in Counseling (ASERVIC) provides a definition and description of spirituality:

> Spirit may be defined as the animating life force, represented by such images as breath, wind, vigor, and courage. Spirituality is the drawing out and infusion of spirit in one's life. It is experienced as an active and passive process. Spirituality is also defined as a capacity and tendency that is innate and unique to all persons. This spiritual tendency moves the individual toward knowledge, love, meaning, peace, hope, transcendence, connectedness, compassion, wellness, and wholeness. Spirituality includes one's capacity for creativity, growth, and the development of a value system. Spirituality encompasses a variety of phenomena, including experiences, beliefs, and practices. Spirituality is approached from a variety of perspectives, including psycho spiritual, religions, and transpersonal. While spirituality is usually expressed through culture, it both precedes and transcends culture. (Steen, Engels, and Thweatt para. 3–4)

Spirituality, in this context, is meant to be encompassing, inclusive and an operational definition for this dissertation. The terms spirituality, spiritual, religious, religiosity, and religion are used interchangeably throughout this study; however, there are times when they may describe divergent meanings. The use of the double term, spirituality/religion, or the phrase the spiritual-religions dimension, is for convenience and ease of reading.

A basic definition of religion is a belief in divine (superhuman or spiritual) beings and the practices (rituals) and moral code (ethics) that are the outcomes of that belief. A belief gives religion its mentality, rituals generate religion's shape, and ethics yield its heart (Gellman and Hartman 10). Another definition for religion is belief in and reverence for a supernatural or higher power recognized as the creator and governor of the universe (i.e., God or a god; Zinn 27). Religion, according to Fukuyama and Sevig, is an organized system of faith, worship, cumulative traditions, and prescribed rituals (233). Religion, as described by Cashwell and Young, provides a social framework wherein a set of beliefs, practices, and experiences manifest (9). Religion can be seen from a perspective as a variety of templates or paradigms through which spirituality is expressed (Grimm 154).

Clinical Considerations

The *Diagnostic and Statistical Manual of Mental Disorders,* fourth edition (DSM-IV™): (American Psychiatric Association) includes a category for religious or spiritual problems that may occur in counseling (685). It is V62.89 Religious or Spiritual Problems for when the focus of clinical attention includes explorations of intense experiences that entail loss or questioning of faith, problems with conversion to a new faith, spiritual awakening, or an examining of other spiritual beliefs that may not necessarily be connected to an organized church or religious institution. The DSM-IV identifies spiritual experiences, crisis, or struggles as a focus of treatment and not per se as a mental disorder or pathology (Cashwell and Young 36). The inclusion of these spiritual-religious issues demonstrates the significance of spirituality and religious aspects in human functioning and the need for their treatment (Burke and Miranti 2).

Ethical Standards

Ethical considerations give rise to arguments both for and against addressing religious and spiritual issues in treatment. Likewise, professional codes of ethics for counselors recognize the importance of the inclusion of religious and spirituality issues with deliberation in the work of counselors (Burke and Miranti 169). The ethical standards of the ACA mandate as a sustaining and beneficial aspect of the counseling process that counselors commit not just to accepting clients, but to increasing their understanding clients' beliefs about the meaning of life, moralities, and worldviews, (Burke and Miranti 169). The code of ethics for counselors is established by professional counseling organizations to make certain that the core values held by members direct professional practice, client services, and due care. Sperry defines a "virtuous therapist" as a professional who possesses good moral character and whose work embodies both the practice of virtue along with the demonstration of professional ethical principles in their daily clinical practice (35).

Counselors' failure to address spiritual and religious issues in counseling may be in some cases considered unethical clinical practice that could be deemed culturally biased (Cashwell and Young 14, 38). However, clinicians need to be mindful of ethical considerations and to adhere within their boundaries of competency based on their education, training, credentials, and experience. Counseling professionals must never practice outside the scope of their boundaries, nor falsely represent expertise or competence in areas in which they are not competent (ACA C.2.a.). Ethical practice mandates proper action with counselors to enlist the support and expertise of colleagues, supervision, and professional consultation with clergy or other spiritual or religious leaders or specialists (Kelly 243–44).

Recently, ethical arguments have been used to support counselors addressing religion and spirituality in counseling under the view that such inclusion can likely promote client growth and well-being. Moreover, religion and spirituality are increasingly embedded within the issues clients bring to therapy (Burke and Miranti 2). First steps for mental health professionals are to provide best practice based on astute clinical protocol and guiding principles regardless of a client's religious or spiritual orientation (Plante 108).

Both the ACA and the American Psychological Association formally acknowledge religion and spirituality in their ethical guidelines as components counselors must consider in their clinical practice (ACA, 4; American

Psychological Association, 2). In Section A.2.c, of the 2005 ACA Code of Ethics, counselors are required to avoid all discrimination based on religion, to increase activity and enhance their understanding of clients with diverse cultural backgrounds, and to reflect upon how their own cultural-ethnic-racial identity has an impact on decisions within the counseling process (ACA 4). In accordance with aforementioned standards related to ethical professional practice, Standard G.1.j of the 2009 Standards of the Council for Accreditation of Counseling and Related Educational Programs requires counselor education programs to orient students to ethical standards enunciated by professional organizations and credentialing bodies that embrace incorporating spirituality into treatment and guiding clients with the use of relevant ethical and legal considerations in counseling practice (10).

II.
Review of the Literature

The review of current professional literature reveals an increasing need to include spirituality and religion in counseling. This research seeks to determine and understand the concepts of spirituality, spiritual practice, and healthy outcomes (Meier, O'Connor, and Vankatwky 43). Sperry cited over 200 published studies indicating that higher levels of spirituality are related to lower risks for psychiatric problems and increased levels of psychosocial functioning. Individuals with elevated levels of spiritual and religious commitment correlate to lower rates of depression symptoms and suicide along with greater levels of wellness and perceived quality of life (25). Empirical research suggests that treatment integrating spirituality and religion appears to boost clients' hopes for recovery, improve clients' self-esteem, and impart positive effects on mental health (Kelly 83).

The major professional associations have conceptualized the significance of spiritual and religious issues in clinical practice (Sperry 194). The counseling literature supports spirituality's central role in human functioning as established by the theoretical and conceptual paradigms (Cashwell and Young 79). Clients are acknowledging and have a desire to explore the spiritual and religious aspects of their lives in therapy, and it is becoming commonplace for clients to communicate openly on the topic (Hughes 1). Spirituality in the counseling process provides options and opportunities for exploration of those values and beliefs that can help to promote growth and wellness (Cashwell and Young 21). To effectively address spiritual concerns in assessment and treatment, counselors need to have certain competencies (Corey 117). Notably, counselors are seeking to implement spirituality into the clinical process (Hinterkopf 1). Many recent publications, both scholarly and in the popular press, have addressed and included strategies for incorporating spirituality and religion into the therapeutic encounter (Richards and Bergin 6).

III.
The Spiritual Competencies

ASERVIC, a division of the ACA, has developed and endorsed fourteen core competencies to help integrate and facilitate spirituality/religion in counseling (n. pag). It is highly recommended that these competencies be pursued by all mental health professionals in clinical practice (Hinterkopf 103). Counseling fundamentals includes training and coursework in the spiritual dimension as a standard curriculum of counselor education programs (Hinterkopf 103). Mattson concurs that in academic programs, students need exposure to religious-spiritual issues to help them comprehend the multicultural issues they are exposed to (191). In addition, ASERVIC recommends that counseling professionals actively engage in exploring their own spirituality in therapy, supervision, classes, workshops, and continuing education hours (Hinterkopf 103). The purpose of establishing these competencies is to assist clinicians in appropriately including spiritual and religious issues in clinical practice (Cashwell and Young ix). ASERVIC's mission is to cultivate ongoing proficiency for this liaison between spirituality/religion and what happens in clinical practice (Cashwell and Young 26).

Culture and Worldview
COMPETENCY 1. *"The professional counselor can describe the similarities and differences between spirituality and religion, including the basic beliefs of various spiritual systems, major world religions, agnosticism, and atheism."* (ASERVIC, n. pag.).

COMPETENCY 2. *"The professional counselor can recognize that the client's beliefs (or absence of beliefs) about spiritu-*

ality and/or religion are central to his or her worldview and can influence psychosocial functioning." (ASERVIC, n. pag.).

Before addressing spirituality or religion in therapy, counselors can benefit from examining their own comfort level (Hughes 3). At the start of therapy, counselors need to build rapport through empathy, trust, warmth, respect, non-judgmental attitude, and acceptance; these attributes are commonly associated with positive outcomes (Richards and Bergin 159). It has become a clinical necessity to consider a client's particular religion or spirituality as a relevant variable in the meaning of clinical issues to the client's life (Lish 2). Kelly asserts that counselors must be informed with a reasonable basic and broad knowledge of the cultural and religious diversity clients may bring to counseling (8). Counselors need to pursue knowledge about world religions, spiritual literacy, and diverse cultures as part of their continuing education and professional development to increase their competency (Cashwell and Young 62).

Bishop outlines specific recommendations for how counselors can work with clients who have diverse religious-spiritual values (qtd. in Burke and Miranti 64). First, counselors need to maintain an open attitude toward clients' religious-spiritual values. Second, counselors are encouraged to consider "a philosophical reorientation" with regard to understanding the functionality of religious-spiritual values as related to clients' cultural make up. In this context, counselors should view religious—spiritual values within a cultural framework (Burke and Miranti 64). Bishop suggests that counselors seek diversified information about clients' cultures, religions/spiritualties, values, beliefs, and practices to decipher how these issues impact and integrate with counseling theory and process (qtd. in Burke and Miranti 66). Counselors are encouraged to seek more knowledge about explicit religious—spiritual ideologies and practices that their clients hold and to observe how such worldviews can influence psychosocial functioning. Primarily, competencies 1 and

2 focus on counselors learning and applying essential religious-spiritual concepts, such as key definitions, similarities, and differences, and examining the exclusive meaning of clients' beliefs and/values (cited in Cashwell and Young 71).

Counselor Self-Awareness

COMPETENCY 3. *"The professional counselor actively explores his or her own attitudes, beliefs, and values about spirituality and/or religion."* (ASERVIC, n.pag.).

COMPETENCY 4. *"The professional counselor continuously evaluates the influence of his or her own spiritual and/or religious beliefs and values on the client and the counseling process."* (ASERVIC, n. pag.).

Kelly states that the integrity of the counseling relationship depends first on counselor awareness and sensitivity along with a nondefensive knowledge of self. This includes having an insightful, honest, undistorted view of oneself and others (90). Counselors' self-awareness establishes an active readiness to enter into a client's world and to view, hear, and explore the client's experience from their frame of reference (Kelly 90). To begin exploration, counselors must first examine and take care of their own spiritual well-being and then, when appropriate, facilitate the enhancement of spirituality for their clients (Richards and Bergin 155).

Within the counseling process, practitioners, the strategy should be to understand and articulate their own experience of spirituality, to model and assist clients in articulating and sharing their own experience, then to integrate within that frame of reference (Meier, O'Connor, and Vankatwky 52). They further point out that the act is first exploring and defining one's own understanding of spirituality. The second step is the interpretation of experience that varies from person to person and is considered a goal of therapy (52). Meier, O'Connor, and Vankatwky describe that experience has a nature and identity of its own and giving voice to one's experience of spirituality is part of the integration process because spirituality is subjective and experiential (52).

A key dynamic to addressing spirituality in counseling is the counselors' self-awareness and consistent assessment of their clinical practice. Counselors who have done the work of exploring and clarifying their personal experience of spirituality have the freedom and competence to begin to incorporate spirituality and religiosity into the therapeutic process with clients, when appropriate (Kelly 43). In addition, counselors need to constantly evaluate and self-monitor the influence of their own spiritual and religious beliefs on the client and the counseling process. Kelly cautions counselors with a spiritual orientation to carefully avoid any unethical practices, directly or indirectly, that would inappropriately influence or impose their own identity and values upon a client (96–97). It is the counselor's responsibility throughout the therapeutic process to be aware of personal beliefs and values, and their influence and affect on clients' treatment and interventions (Kelly 97).

COMPETENCY 5. *"The professional counselor can identify the limits of his or her understanding of the client's spiritual and/or religious perspectives and is acquainted with religious and spiritual resources and leaders who can be avenues for consultation and to whom the counselor can refer."* (ASERVIC, n. pag.).

Kelly asserts that it is crucial for counselors to recognize and identify their own limitations as their clients work through challenging religious and spiritual matters within the counseling process (100). Cashwell and Young contend that the focal point of Competency 5 is to coordinate counselor's self-awareness garnered from Competency 3 to combine it with the knowledge and awareness derived from Competency 4 to prepare counselors for when their own professional aptitude does not match a client's need (84). The competent counselor recognizes the limits of clinical training and knowledge in treating a client's spiritual or religious concerns and recognizes when to consult or make an appropriate referral (Cashwell and Young 32). This decision comes from counselors' frank appraisal of their own limitations and ethical considerations based on the clients' needs and issues. When dealing with an concern that cannot be met by the therapist, a consultation or referral would be in the best interest of the client (Cashwell and Young 86). According to Plante, mental health professionals are not required or expected to be experts on spiritual-religious matters to help clients (57). There are available resources for practitioners to consult with other specialists: clergy, holistic centers, churches and temples, faith-spiritual associations and communities, and other service providers who can be utilized for a client's benefit (Plante 81).

The essential protocol in clinical practice is that counselors maintain professional relationships and alliances with local and community spiritual and religious leaders who can provide consultation and referrals through cooperative collaboration (Cashwell and Young 86). Moreover, counselors need to heed the limits of their professional roles with clear boundaries and interventions: They must not perform functions that should be assumed by clergy or spiritual leaders, nor practice outside their area of competence (Plante 43). For a consultation to be successful, first the professional referral must be appropriate to best meet a client's need. Second, the client must feel secure that the professional is actually capable and qualified to deploy and validate the referral (Cashwell and Young 89). Faiver et al. support counseling professionals' need to create a comprehensive consultation and referral resource list with members of different faiths and spiritual communities who are highly skilled, well-known, and respected in local communities. They should respect and understand what counselors do and understand the counseling dynamics. Then as an added bonus, they should be educated about coursework related to the counseling profession for efficient networking opportunities (qtd. in Cashwell and

Young 89–90).

Human and Spiritual Development
COMPETENCY 6. *"The professional counselor can describe and apply various models of spiritual and/or religious development and their relationship to human development."* (ASERVIC, n. pag.).

Various theories and disciplines shape our understanding of human development and maturation through the life cycle (Clark and Caffarella 20). The time-honored classic theories focus on stage or phase development; others highlight life events and transitions, and the newer theoretical models focus on gender identity, development, and the sociocultural perspective. These all shape the developmental intricacies of how we grow and develop as individuals (Clark and Caffarella 6). Theories of human and spiritual development need to honor a client's experiences, since the journey through one's life cycle is molded by psychological, social, physical, and mental influences whereby the spiritual and religious tenets within lifespan development evoke different outcomes for different individuals with positive, negative, and often mixed results (Kelly 68–69). Theories of human and spiritual development can provide a conceptual map or lens for discovery, insight, and revelation to elaborate the endeavor of becoming human, a lifelong quest and developmental process (Clark and Caffarella 26). Ingersoll postulates that spirituality has evolved to be understood as a construct of human development (qtd. in Burke and Miranti 15).

Kelly stipulates that counselors need to be knowledgeable the spiritual-religious dimension's influence on developmental perspectives over the lifespan (68). This is due to counseling's profound roots in the conception of human growth and development (Cashwell and Young 33). Within the growth of faith, spirituality, morality, or values is a component of human development that can be reinforced by the therapeutic interventions and counseling process (Kelly 68–69). Alert counselors need to identify and understand that the major domains of human development—cognitive, psychosocial, ego, moral, and spiritual—are interrelated and interconnected. Counselors also need to be cognizant and recognize that a client's current spiritual or religious outlook may include conditions of an earlier developmental stage or challenges, as well as clients' differing levels of spiritual development (Cashwell and Young 33, 107). Cashwell and Young endorse that competent clinicians not only prescribe and apply assorted models of spiritual development and transformation, but they also take it to the next level by comparing and contrasting the models for appraisal and integration into their approach and theory of counseling (114).

Case Example

This case deals with a divorced white male client age 36, struggling with his religious beliefs, severe depression, and the will to live. He had no current involvement with church or God. He had suffered a chronic condition that could have killed him, survived, and needed to create a new life, because the one he had had was no longer relevant. He believed that God had spared him; but for what since the life he had known was gone. He had lived a full life: travel all over the world, expensive vacations, money in the bank, women, and whatever he wanted; now it was dead. The client had become disabled, was applying for SSI, and was incapable of living on his own. Nor could he do the building construction work he loved. He was forced to live with his parents after being away from home for over ten years. The client was in the grips of a spiritual crisis when he was advised by his doctor to seek therapy. He selected a Catholic agency; this was unconscious, but later proved crucial to his treatment. Not knowing what to expect from therapy, he came seeking and questioning.

Initially, the client put no emphasis on his faith, since it had been inactive for many years. His mother was a devoted Catholic and immersed in the church, its practices, and her prayers for him. He was in limbo in his spiritual development, still stuck in his beliefs and his identify as a self-made man. He questioned what God had to do with his successes and the grand lifestyle he had acquired. In therapy, we identify that he was a mature adult with the power of choice and exploration to determine what his beliefs held for him as he sought meaning from his illness. He began a search to find himself on a journey of self-discovery to connect to something bigger than himself. My client knew that God existed because he had survived, and he was able to acknowledge that it was truly a miracle. He should have died and somehow God gave him a second chance. In treatment, we worked on developing a "new normal" for him; what is impossible with man is possible with God. He just needed a vision and the faith to frame what he wanted for his life. So he reexamined his faith and belief system to revamp them; he went back to church on his own, first to bible study and then regular church. He spoke with his family priest for guidance, as well as in his search for answers. He began reading the bible for himself and journaling, which revealed profound content; through this process he uncovered the strength and spirit that was always within him. The client started to dream again, and he took one college course, and then he decided to pursue his bachelor's degree, something that he always wanted to do, but had no time for when he was working. He used to live for only work and the pleasures. Now, he wanted to give back from this second chance at living fully his life: body, mind, and spirit. He even became a volunteer at a local medical center and gave his testimony to anyone that would listen to him in gratitude for the value of life and his spiritual awakening. This client's mindset changed through the human and spiritual development of his old thoughts and old dogmas to begin life as a new man in his personal walk with God. He let the former things pass away and began seeing himself in a new light. This client became whole and functional despite his health limitations; he was discharged from therapy after a year of treatment. The client's spiritual development evolved so that he could move forward with newness of life and be transformed. It was a rewarding process to witness as the therapist: my and client's finest hour.

Communication

COMPETENCY 7. *"The professional counselor responds to client communications about spirituality and/or religion with acceptance and sensitivity."* (ASERVIC, n. pag.).

COMPETENCY 8. *"The professional counselor uses spiritual and/or religious concepts that are consistent with the client's spiritual and/or religious perspectives and are acceptable to the client."* (ASERVIC, n. pag.).

COMPETENCY 9. *"The professional counselor can recognize spiritual and/or religious themes in client communication and is able to address these with the client when they are therapeutically relevant."* (ASERVIC, n. pag.).

Counselors initiate the engagement to address a client's religious and spiritual perspectives within the therapeutic process to create an environment of openness and sincerity (Cashwell and Young 34, 122). Kelly explains that the counseling relationship forms a humanistic bond, a healing partnership between the counselor and client, which requires potent aptitude: the practitioner's responsiveness to clients that cultivates effective interpersonal and communications skills (88, 100). Counselors need be alert to client's self-exploration of spiritual and religious materials, while creating collaboration to enable responsiveness and acceptance throughout the course of the counseling process (Kelly 110). Counselors need to review respectfully the spiritual-religious dynamics that are significantly therapeutically relevant, positively or negatively connected to the issues and problems clients bring to therapy (Cashwell and Young 34).

Likewise, counselors need to be aware of the concepts, terms, and language of clients' "spiritual conceptualization" within clients' own frame of reference using various communication techniques to facilitate the therapeutic alliance (Cashwell and Young 124). Hughes affirms that counselors should be aware of a client's spiritual vocabulary where words have different nuances and implications. It is appropriate for the counselor to probe cautiously and inquire as to meaning using the client's own specifiers (4). Effective communication relies on the interactions and rapport established between counselor and client that are essential to attaining treatment success, in conjunction with diligent attention to clients' spiritual and religious dimensions when pertinent (Cashwell and Young 135). Hinterkopf stipulates that counselors need to copy the client's language when working with spiritual issues (78). The important factor is that words are powerful, and practitioners need to be sensitive to client use and discourse without judging or classifying them (Cunningham 21). "It is the client who knows what hurts, what directions to go, what problems are crucial, what experiences are deeply buried."—Carl Rogers

Assessment

COMPETENCY 10. *"During the intake and assessment processes, the professional counselor strives to understand a client's spiritual and/or religious perspectives by gathering information from the client and/or other sources."* (ASERVIC n. pag).

The assessment comes first before clinicians can feasibly introduce or incorporate religious or spiritual interventions into the counseling process (Plante 64). Counselors begin with an appropriate assessment to develop a better sense of clients' religious-spiritual matters that may or may not affect their work with clients (Plante 49). Sperry concurs that clinicians initiate an inquiry about the place of God, religion, church, community, and spiritual practices in their client's lives. Clinicians, through the initial inquiry need to assess the degree and influence of religion and spirituality in clients' feelings, thoughts, and behavior (136). One of the objectives of the assessment is to differentiate healthy from pathological religious experiences (Sperry 22).

The intake is the first step towards inclusion of the religious—spiritual dimension in the assessment process with an initial exploratory phase which sets the climate for the client or counselor to bring forth the relevance or irrelevance of religion and spirituality (Cashwell and Young 153). An attuned counselor can develop a better understanding of the role that religion and spirituality play in clients' lives in consort with both their constructive and destructive influences using Pulchlski and Rommer' this one simple approach called FICA (qtd. in Plante 58). The name denotes four key terms: Faith, Importance, Church, and Address. The approach pertains to counselors asking this specific set of questions: faith (What is your faith, if any?), importance (How important is your faith?), church (What is your church or community, if any?) and address (How would you like me to address these issues in your treatment? Plante 58). These informal questions can lead to an operational exchange for further inquiry and discussion as needed throughout the course of treatment. For the client, the assessment can increase self-exploration and self-awareness to promote growth and progression; for the counselor the spiritual assessment is a vital device for formulating and enhancing a positive therapeutic collaboration (Cashwell and Young 142).

Diagnosis and Treatment

COMPETENCY 11. *"When making a diagnosis, the professional counselor recognizes that the client's spiritual and/or religious perspectives can a) enhance well-being; b) contribute to client problems; and/or c) exacerbate symptoms"* *(ASERVIC n. pag).*

COMPETENCY 12. *"The professional counselor sets goals with the clients that are consistent with the client's spiritual and/or religious perspectives"* *(ASERVIC n.pag).*

COMPETENCY 13. *"The professional counselor is able to a) modify therapeutic techniques to include a client's spiritual and/or religious perspectives, and b) utilize spiritual and/or religious practices as techniques when appropriate and acceptable to a client's viewpoint"* (ASER VIC n. pag).

A competent counselor, right from the beginning of the counseling encounter, is appraising the client's assets and traits (Cashwell and Young 144). Through the assessment process, counselors are not just focusing on a client's presenting issue or a client's spiritual or religious matters, but the integration of spirituality as part of a holistic perspective exploring the whole person which includes physical, emotional, spiritual, and environmental dimensions (Cashwell and Young 144). Kelly suggests that once the intake is complete, then the second task is to deal with a client's initial self-exploration of concern or indifference towards the spiritual-religious dimension (153). In addition, Sperry gives a key rationale for counselors to perform spiritual assessment that appraises a client's spiritual-religious well-being; its influence on the presenting issues, crises, and disturbances; and whether the client's spiritual belief systems and resources may be used for healing and coping skills (111). Afterwards, counselors assess a client's spiritual orientation and then evaluate whether or not to address a client's spiritual needs and/or issues in therapy. Next, the counselor deliberates regarding which type of spiritual interventions or practices to use as techniques and identify objectives for treatment goals that would be appropriate to serve the client's best interest (Sperry 111). This speaks to Competency 12, setting goals that are consistent with the client's spiritual and religious orientations.

Counseling treatment mandates a functional level of diagnostic propriety and treatment planning, as necessity for mental health services and third-party reimbursements (Jongsma, Peterson, and Bruce 1). Therefore when using a spiritual framework, it is necessary to understand the dynamics of spirituality/religion in conjunction with diagnostic interpretation and implementation. Counselors need to be aware of transformational spiritual experiences when the experience could provide evidence of spiritual emergence that produces growth and positive transformation. This could become part of one's daily life or, in other circumstances, turn out to be spiritual emergencies with mental health symptoms and pathology (Cashwell and Young 164). Counselors without a grasp of transformational spiritual experiences may be guided to diagnose a client with pathology for a genuine spiritual experience rather than view their experience within a spiritual or religious context (Cashwell and Young 164). Cashwell and Young contend that while psychological issues must be distinguished from transpersonal experiences, the key is balancing the data and recognizing when clients have genuine mental health issues that warrant diagnosis, medication evaluations, and treatment. This balance comes with a working awareness of spiritual transformations that can frequently contain mental health symptoms (165). Counselors can run the risk of promoting pathology to a religious experience or subverting spiritual transformation by assessing pathology (Cashwell and Young 165). Lastly, the competent and ethically minded counselor considers a client's spiritual-religious orientation, then makes accurate diagnosis and formulates treatment plans that are appropriate, therapeutic, and acceptable to a client's viewpoint (Cashwell and Young 165). This addresses Competency 13, as it speaks to the counselor's proficiency to modify therapeutic techniques and interventions in concert with the client's spirituality and religiosity.

Counselors must make appropriate use of theories and current research to address and support integration of a client's spiritual-religious orientation in counseling. Therefore, diagnosis and treatment planning, which also includes recommendation for counseling is based on a client's overall clinical presentation, and addresses the client's greatest needs (Jongsma, Peterson, and Bruce 4) A crucial step in treatment planning is the creation of goals and objectives. Goals are usually global and long term to denote a desired positive outcome. Objectives must be stated in clear, behaviorally measurable language to determine whether the client has achieved the outcome. Each objective is a step toward reaching the overall treatment goal and is consistent with the client's belief system. The actions of the clinician are the intervention used to help the client complete the objectives. The interventions are created based on a client's needs and the clinician's range of therapeutic practice and theological perspectives. The diagnosis determination is based on the therapist's familiarity with the DSM-IV (Jongsma, Peterson, and Bruce 3). In the case of the spiritual-religious domains, there are times where counseling goals are less specific and nonbehavioral (Cashwell and Young 173). This is a collaborative effort and is performed with the client; the clinician and client will share the work of developing goals for the treatment plan (Cashwell and Young 172).

COMPETENCY 14. *"The professional counselor can therapeutically apply theory and current research supporting the inclusion of a client's spiritual and/or religious perspectives and practices" (ASERVIC n.pag).*

Competency 14 addresses the application of theory and current research to support the inclusion of a client's spiritual and religious orientation and practices in counseling. Plante identifies three principles to help mental health professionals maximize the success of research: a) learn from success, b) benefit from creative collaboration, and c) establish useful resources and networks (177). Plante states that one of the best examples is the research on mindfulness-based stress reduction. The mindfulness approach has become an acceptable and conventional intervention approach for a variety of clinical issues and is supported by empirical proof and grounded research conducted at prestigious university and medical-center settings by seasoned researchers (Plante 177). Plante states that the growing research literature in religion/spirituality benefits from collaborative pursuits that provide opportunities for mentorship and networking, and allow learning from each other on a grand scale (178). Finally, Plante points out that the funding sources that provide financial support for research involving religious and spiritual practices—which may include federal grants, foundation grants, or private foundations—have offered to liberally fund research and training (179). There are ongoing collaborations with researchers building collective teams with clergy and other religious/spiritual communities for the clinical care of clients, including research and study possibilities and prospects to develop beneficial resources and networks (179). These principles demonstrate the ways that research can impact what mental health professionals do in actual clinical practice.

IV.
Spiritual Frameworks

Holistic Approach

The holistic approach involves a need or hunger to be understood as a whole person (Cunningham 19). The term holistic is focused on the whole person—one of three features: the mind, body, and spirit (Cashwell and Young 26). Counseling values a holistic approach to clinical practice, whereby clients are understood as biological, psychological, social, and spiritual, with a focus on wholeness and growth (Cunningham 19). According to Gross, the concept of holistic health is an approach to wellness; where prevention and alternative ways of treating illness or disorders are included so good health and the full enjoyment of life can be realized (96). For the counselor, the process involves engaging the whole person of the client through interventions conducive to a wholesome lifestyle and inclusive of a variety of activities, such as meditation, diet and exercise, emotional vivacity, and spirituality (Gross 100). Hughes affirms this option to address spirituality in psychotherapy via a holistic criterion that comprises the body-mind-emotional-spiritual connection. The client is viewed as one psychosomatic whole—spirit, intellect, and body (7).

Soul Care

Soul care has emerged with renewed interest in the field of psychology, and in the practice of counseling and psychotherapy, its composition has been deliberated through the ages in philosophic circles (Uomoto n. pag.). Soul care is an old ideal of a soul-centered world that originates with the ancient philosophers and theologians. Plato expressed in the *Charmides* (quoting the Thracian King Zamolxis): "as you ought not to attempt to cure the eyes without the head, or the head without the body, so neither ought you attempt to cure the body without the soul...for the part can never be well unless the whole is well...and therefore if the head and body are to be well, you must begin by curing the soul" (qtd. in Jowett I.6). The ancients consider the soul as the crux of human experience, as acknowledged by Plotinus: "for the soul is the beginning of all things. It is the soul that lends all things movement" (qtd. in Uomoto n. pag.). Today, as we consult our past history, we deal with the same issues in need of a rebirth of ancient wisdom and practice to accommodate life in the twenty-first century (Moore xvi).

Uomoto embraces the current preamble of soul care, which now has new significance as a viable and vital means of healing emotional suffering and dealing with meaninglessness that surfaces with human finitude (n. pag.). Soul care hopes to find a point of convergence between counseling and spirituality to shoulder the human condition (Uomoto, n. pag.). Thereby, counseling could be enhanced for some clients wrestling with soul care issues, the opportunities to find meaning and purpose through spiritual sojourning. Soul care pays attention to the care of persons in their totality and of their inner life; it is an approach for the whole person: body, soul, and spirit. Soul-focused interventions are developed to help clients to go deeper into their experiences, to see the difficulties and work through unresolved issues

The "loss of soul" is when the soul is neglected and we have lost the wisdom of the soul (Moore xii). Consequently, as clinicians, we help our clients to focus on how to foster living soulfully in everyday life (Moore xvi). Moore outlines the emotional ailments that therapists hear daily in clinical practice: emptiness; meaninglessness; vague depression; disillusionment about marriage, family, and relationships; a loss of values; yearning for personal fulfillment; and a hunger for spirituality (xvi). He further points out that all these symptoms echo a loss of soul, the longings and cravings of the soul (xvi). The care of the soul begins with its manifestations, and operations. Moore gives us the origins in the Latin *cura;* while *cura* is commonly translated as care, it actually contains the idea of both care and cure (5). Care refers to ongoing actions designed to support the well-being of something or someone. While cure refers to actions that restore lost well-being: as the problem is solved, the patient is cured (18). Soul care involves nurturing and support as well as healing and restoration; care that taps into the deepest level of people's inner lives. Soul care promotes care that has a sense of ongoing attention, where there is no end, because sometimes conflicts and problems may never be fully resolved (Moore 19).

The care of the soul requires that we live our lives for the good of the soul. It is an inner working; an inside job related to total personhood, which is attached to what actually happens, the good, the bad, and the ugly that cultivates a meaningful life (Moore 5). Care of the soul involves "work" that could be inspiring but often it is very challenging to take the honest path to visit emotions; we do not want to feel and to gain insight and understanding of what we would prefer to do without (Moore 291). It is the ordinary things we practice each day that are fundamental to the soul; look for the "epiphanies" (Moore 288). Moore declares that care of the soul reaches another realm, as we care soulfully by honoring its expressions and lessons, giving time for revelations and living life that cultivates as much from the heart as from the head (304). "The soul has its own purpose and end" (Moore 304). Moore interprets that some type of spiritual life is absolutely necessary for psychological "health," within normality (xii).

Spiritual Wellness and Well-Being

Myers defines spiritual wellness as "a continuing search for meaning and purpose in life: an appreciation for depth of life, the expanse of the universe, and natural forces which operate: a personal belief system" (11). Opatz states in this way that a person who is spiritually well seeks harmony between what lies within the individual and what lies outside of the individual (qtd. in Chandler, Holden, and Kolander 168). Within a wellness framework, spirituality is a natural part of being human that can be conceptualized though practicality. Ellison and Smith state that well-being "reflects the proper functioning of persons as integrated systems" (36). Health and wholeness therefore, are correlated and key for healthy human functioning and positive and affirming adjustment (36). Well-being is defined as a comprehensive concept that includes general satisfaction with life and a sense of peace, as well as comfort with one's place or position in the world. It entails a sense of achievement, positive self-esteem, and collective values and behaviors (Plante 18). Chandler, Holden, and Kolander describe that counseling for spiritual wellness is a viable pursuit for counselors and clients, as spirituality is inherent within all humans. Spiritual wellness is not an obscure or a vague concept (174). Chandler, Holden, and Kolander challenge counselors to be willing to work in the spiritual dimension in order to provide a venue that possesses both spiritual and personal modalities for transformation and processing of mental and spiritual growth that can achieve higher levels of wellness. Counselors by nature are inherently the promoters of human development and likely sponsors for the advancement of spiritual wellness (174).

V.
Spiritual Intervention Techniques

The intervention phase is the heart of therapy; it is the center of insight, discovery, change, growth, and healing (Cunningham 55). The following seven techniques with general descriptions may help to cultivate the discussion of spiritual issues and also lend themselves to working in the spiritual dimension. Spiritual techniques can be used in therapy to help clients cope, heal, and grow (Richards and Bergin 251). As interventions during a treatment session or as homework assignments, spiritual activities and practices can be a formidable addition to the treatment process (Sperry 147).

Prayer

Prayer as a spiritual activity is perhaps the most distinguishing and characteristic element of the spiritual dimension (Sperry 152). Sperry states that prayer is essential to most spiritual seekers; most clients pray on occasion and many use prayer as a means of coping with life's challenges (152). In nearly all spiritual and religious traditions, the value of prayer is acknowledged based on the integrity and genuineness of the pray-er (Kelly 225). Cashwell and Young assert that, for many people, prayer is a governing spiritual practice (243). A believer's prayers take on many forms for example: thanksgiving, honor/praise, intercession, petition, confession/repentance, forgiveness, and invocation (Richards and Bergin 253). Research indicates the value of regular prayer, its significant healing power, and a variety of benefits including enhanced psychological functioning, increased well-being, a sense of meaning and fulfillment, stress reduction and improved coping (Plante 33).

It is important to note that many clients are engaging in a

prayerful life regardless of whether the counselor addresses that fact (Cashwell and Young 243). Prayer, therefore, is occurring whether or not the counselor is aware of it, whether or not the counselor considers it significant, and whether or not the counselor wants to deal with it (Cashwell and Young 243). Kelly stipulates that the role of prayer in secular counseling is controversial and problematic (226). Counselors need to be careful and consider ethical issues, dual relationships, professional boundaries, and unhealthy transference issues while using prayer in the clinical context (Richards and Bergin 254). Sperry lists four versions of healing prayers encountered by therapists in clinical practice: first and most controversial, in-session direct prayer with clients; second, prayer that occurs outside of therapy; third, clinicians praying for guidance on treatment/diagnosis; and, fourth, allowing the client to pray in-session while the clinician sits in silence (152). Richards and Bergin offer some precautionary tips for mental health professionals when considering prayer with their clients during a therapy session: consider the setting of the practice; consider the type of client, devout or higher functioning; execute within the client's religious or spiritual orientation, and, when needed, provide appropriate referrals to religious leaders or communities (254). McCullough and Larson assert that praying with clients should only happen when three conditions converge: a) It is at the client's request for prayer. b) The therapist is careful to keep therapeutic boundaries to avoid the potential for dual relationships. c) Competent clinical care is practiced within appropriate ethical boundaries (qtd. in Richards and Bergin 254).

Forgiveness
Forgiveness, next to prayer may be the most commonly applied spiritual practice. Plante suggests that the practice of forgiveness is one of the spiritual interventions most used by therapist (91; Richards and Bergin 264). Research reveals that forgiveness is an essential element of interpersonal and psychological healing (Richards and Bergin 264). The value

of forgiveness is recognized by most spiritual traditions (Sperry 155). Schimmel states, "forgiveness is prosocial," a multifaceted process that encompasses thoughts, feelings, and sometimes actions towards a culpable transgressor (qtd. in Cunningham 77). Forgiveness is not a one-time event, however, it is an ongoing transforming and healing process for the offended person (Kelly 219). There are some healing benefits of forgiveness: release of the pain brought on by the anger and resentment we feel when maltreated and inner peace from the anger relinquished (Cunningham 77). Kelly contends that forgiveness has an affiliation with religious practice, but it is also appropriate for counselors with a "general positively value" to support the merits of forgiveness (219). Richards and Bergin hold that forgiveness can be encouraged and sanctioned with no reference to religious or spiritual tenets (264).

Richards and Bergin caution therapists that before they begin to encourage clients to forgive others or seek forgiveness, it is essential that they first assess client appropriateness and preparedness for such intervention. They outline that clients most often need to go through a healing process: a) acknowledgement; b) awareness and recognition of the abuse and offense; c) experiencing and expressing feelings of hurt, grief, and anger; d) getting validation that they have been wronged and, if possible, receiving justice and restitution; e) having boundary repair (that the abuse or offenses will not happen again); and f) moving on with life after letting go and forgiving (265). Clinicians must give clients ample opportunity to work through each phrase discernibly, because forgiveness involves a process of reconciliation that takes time, time for the healing process to avoid damage or premature outcomes that could do more harm than good (Richards and Bergin 265).

Meditation

Meditation, like prayer has many forms, and it is a spiritual practice. Many of religious-spiritual traditions offer distinct types of meditation practices. Meditation has been adopted into the counseling and psychotherapy process as an intervention for alleviating assorted mental, emotional, and physical problems, including stress (Kelly 222). Meditation is described as of form of relaxation that enhances awareness, by centering and focusing on the self (Sperry 158). Meditation has been found to enhance psychological health, well-being, and mental and physical functioning (Plante 72). Vital research has meticulously demonstrated that meditation helps to promote relaxation, and practices that involve religious—spiritual convictions lead to even greater health benefits (Plante 73). One excellent example of a meditative technique used with therapy is a mantra, usually a focus of attention. A *mantra* is a short phrase or a few key words associated with one's familiarity of the sacred or a holy name within a religious tradition or consciousness. There are some key elements present for meditation practice: a quiet place, a specific, comfortable posture or position, a focus of attention and an open attitude that allows distractions to come and go without judgment (Sutton 330). Practitioners may recommend meditation when it is appropriate and matches a client's religious—spiritual tenets (Plante 74). Clients practicing meditation may be able to change how they regulate the ebb and flow of their emotions and their thinking to achieve physical relaxation, psychological harmony, and wellness (Sutton 329–30).

Mindfulness

Mindfulness is the opposite of mindlessness, operating on "automatic pilot," unaware of current experience or not in touch with "here and now" (Cashwell and Young 186). According to Cashwell and Young mindfulness is not a technique or skill: it is a way of being (195). It can be practiced within meditation; here it is described on its own, as it can be practiced outside of the formal practice of meditation (Sperry 162). Mindfulness is experiencing the world in the "here and now," this mode is referred to as the *being* mode: being in the present moment, and fully participating moment to moment (Sperry 162). Mindfulness is the practice of being in the present moment, without judgment. Being mindful means seeing life and experiencing life as it is (Cashwell and Young 185).

It sounds simple enough, but it is hard to achieve because of our human psyche and own natural habits, tendencies of seeing things through the lens of the past and habits (Cashwell and Young 186). Mindfulness is experiential; it involves informal and formal observations without attachment to an assumed viewpoint (Cashwell and Young 186). Germer offers three forms of mindfulness: a) awareness, b) presence, and c) acceptance (qtd. in Cashwell and Young 186). He contends that all three parts are interconnected, but the presence of one aspect does not require the presence of others. Mindfulness is simply noticing what is occurring in the present moment with intention, attention, and openness without judgment (Cashwell and Young 186). Mindfulness, the art of "being present," can help clients focus on one thing at a time to be fully in the moment, not thinking about the past, the future, themselves, or their emotions in a negative way. Speaking directly to mindfulness, Abraham Maslow said, "The ability to be in the present moment is a major component of mental wellness."

Journal Writing

Journal writing is used by many in therapeutic settings, and it can be used to explore a client's spiritual orientation. There are many benefits to journal writing in reducing stress, helping with organization, setting goals and resolutions, focusing, and increasing awareness. Moreover, it is a safe place for introspection and self-discovery (qtd. in Cunningham 59). The objective in journal writing is self-discovery or an exploration of the divine (qtd. in Cunningham 59). Journal writing helps clients get in touch with emotions and vent feelings, as well as channel self-reflection that can motivate positive changes. Hughes affirms that journal writing could be useful as an intervention to help clients to explore their inner consciousness of spirituality through dialoguing with the higher self or one's notion of God (6). Journaling is a private act. However, clients may share entries with their therapist as they wish; it is their choice (Cunningham 59).

Spiritual Reading

Sacred writings are viewed by major Eastern and Western spiritual traditions as a source of spiritual and moral wisdom (Sperry 161). The Bible remains the best-selling book in America. Reading of the Bible and other scriptures, sacred and common literature, is encouraged by spiritual-religious traditions and church communities to enhance spiritual life (Plante 36). Bible studies, stories, and biographies of important religious figures are also used to help interested parties grow in faith and knowledge of biblical traditions and principles (Plante 36). Reading sacred texts—for example, the Bible, Torah, or Koran, as well as other written annotations and literature—is a useful tool for therapists (Plante 78). Job in the bible is a prime example of pain and suffering that led to depression and despair. He lost everything he had, his wife, children, cattle and health. Yet, Job remained loyal to God during his tribulation. In the end, because he endured, Job was restored more than what he had in the beginning due to his faith in God. The story of Job, who is the central character of the book of Job, is found in the Old Testament of the bible. Many other people throughout the bible can be used to illustrate how to deal with the problem of depression.

Due to differing traditions and individual needs, the reasons for reading sacred writings can vary (Sperry 161). Some will read and study traditional sacred writings for knowledge or to increase their understanding of ideology, theology, or philosophy; others will read for comfort, answers, insights, and meaning (Sperry 161). Still other individuals study to usher themselves into the very presence of the divine (Sperry 161). These sacred writings are used for multiple purposes in spiritual-religious therapy. Richards and Bergin refer to the following purposes: to challenge or modify dysfunctional beliefs, to reframe and comprehend life and problems from a spiritual viewpoint, to clarify or enrich the meaning of religious principles, and to seek enlightenment, solace, and direction (qtd, in Sperry 161). Clinicians must carefully assess clients' beliefs and attitudes before implementing sacred writings as a spiritual intervention, and only use this when it is attuned with the client's needs and beliefs (Sperry 161). As emphasized, clinicians should remain within their area of competence and be ready to refer clients to members of the clergy or other religious experts to help with their questions, inquiries, or the interpretation of sacred writings (Plante 78).

Bibliotherapy

Bibliotherapy is an educational intervention using texts, novels, poems, movies, and other media as therapeutic assignments. Encouraging clients to read books or self-help materials that can augment their treatment and self-care is long-standing practice and a useful tool for counselors (Plante 78). The counselor selects or recommends such texts or reading materials based on a client's specific needs. Then, through discovery and review, clients are able to gain some clarity, insights, and awareness to problem solve and reach their goals. Sperry asserts that counselors must follow up on the readings they assign to process the content with the client for their impressions and comprehension of the material (143). The counselor should have prior knowledge of the recommended materials. The counselors, if possible, and appropriate can read or watch along with the client during a therapy session (Harper and McFadden 287).

The practice of bibliotherapy begins with the intentional selection and use of literature, media, or movies, followed by the careful processing and review with the client (Harper and McFadden 285). Reading becomes an avenue for change and transformation when applied therapeutically. For the process to be successful, professionals who subscribe to the specialty of bibliotherapy have identified four phases that clinicians should follow. Phase 1 is the identification step: the therapist identifies client issues. Phases 2 and 3 include multiple steps: knowledge of the client's reading level, timing, a method of presenting the intervention or homework assignment, and the selection of appropriate and relevant materials. Finally, Phrase 4 is the follow-up to process the activity for reflection and meaning with the client (Harper and McFadden 285). It is important for the counselor to be aware of the client's experiences of reading or watching videos, since that would affect the use of bibliotherapy. The objective of bibliotherapy is to help clients develop a better understanding of themselves, others, or other issues, to gain insights that inspire growth and wellness (Plante 78).

Integration
It can be helpful for clinicians to inquire about the spiritual practices, habits, rituals, or customs the client follows. Clinicians need to ask about the frequency, duration, and the impact or effect of these practices on their life (Sperry 114). Counselors need to prepare appropriately when integrating and incorporating spiritual interventions into the counseling dynamic by equipping themselves with an arsenal of specific strategies (Sperry 138). According to Sperry, clinicians need a repertoire of flexible techniques. He suggests a therapeutic use of self (the clinician's own spiritual journey and process), an understanding of the spiritual dimension (how it is handled explicitly or implicitly), and proper utilization and timing of interventions (prayer, spiritual readings, spiritual bibliotherapy, forgiveness, and meditation) along with other practices and resources (138). These spiritual interventions need to be assessed to match a client's ability and the presenting issues, problems, and goals (Cunningham 55). The main objective of spiritual interventions in counseling is to help promote the process of transformation or the ongoing tweaking and growth within a holistic framework that encompasses psychological, moral, and somatic features (Sperry 14). Sperry encourages clinicians to use their own ingenuity and ongoing experiences with spiritual interven-

tions for clients. This can result in conceptualizing other strategies and approaches to incorporate the spiritual dimension in therapy (143). Cunningham proposes that counselors go beyond just symptom alleviation: spiritual interventions should draw on clients' strengths to provide wholeness and growth in harmony with their religious—spiritual beliefs (56–57). Clinicians should only use spiritual interventions within their competency that are appropriate for clients with intact egos (Cunningham 56). Therapeutic gifts and spiritual interventions offer several outcomes: increased self-awareness, enhanced relationships, enriched self-esteem, authentic living, and perfected self-efficacy (Cunningham 159).

Case Study

The client is a divorced, 43-year-old white female; she lives alone and has one child, who is estranged. The client's presenting issues was her recent divorce, and unresolved grief issues brought on by the death of her ex-husband. Struggling to discover new meaning in her intense response to this loss while restructuring her life, she decided to seek therapy. The client was open to exploring her spirituality and she agreed to several different spiritual interventions: prayer, bibliotherapy, and journal writing. These interventions were fine and client did follow through with various homework assignments. However, when client continued to experience overwhelming loss and emptiness, it was assessed that she needed a connection to something more. The client's social and family contacts were limited by her own choosing. She was a loner and through the course of treatment when the therapist suggested that she could benefit from some type of support group, but she adamantly refused to consider it. Meanwhile, as her mourning persisted, she became angry and upset at the lack of emotional support and understanding from family and friends. The therapist reintroduced the idea of joining a support group and provided several different opportunities for client to pursue it. The timing was right and the client agreed. She tried out several different groups before she found her match. She attended a Divorce Care group and a grief support group provided by different local churches. The client shared that her experiences with the two groups were very helpful, communal, and informative. She met wonderful people and was able to reestablish some basic social contact with others that diminished her isolation and expanded her support network with individuals that could empathize with her struggles and feelings about her grief/loss. This was very curative for the client and she has since been able to move forward through the various tasks of mourning.

Another issue the client faced during her spiritual crisis was her own church's feeble response to her bereavement. She found the strength to confront her pastor, but was not satisfied with his reaction. She mustered the courage to visit other local churches in her quest for a better spiritual community, discovering and joining a new church that better met her needs. She made new friends and connected to others, while preparing to get involved in one of the church's ministries. The client is creating a new life for herself; she has taken bold steps towards healing, recovery, and transformation. Another great leap was the client's decision to stay in the home she once shared with her deceased ex-spouse, now newly renovated with her personal decor selections. This client has been freed to embark on a new life in a way that honors her relationship with her ex-husband. She believes that he would be pleased and so proud of her efforts. As her therapist, it has been exhilarating to witness this client's tremendous progress, renewal, and spiritual transformation. A quote from Albert Bandura sums up this case: "By sticking it out through tough times, people emerge from adversity with a stronger sense of efficacy."

VI.
Clients' Spiritual Typology

Mental health professionals will find different types of clients in various clinical situations: clients who are very religious, clients who have been damaged by their religious traditions or leaders, clients struggling with religious beliefs and traditions, clients who are not religious, clients outside the therapist's religious tradition, and clients with destructive religious views and behaviors (Plante 116). Each client offers a unique narrative and set of life circumstances that challenges counselors to provide competent services tailored to the needs of the individual (Plante 116). Kelly points out that clients can and do change characteristics from one identifiable orientation to another. Also, he notes that characteristics do overlap and there are various assortments of client attitudes, behaviors, and practices, so clinicians need to take caution and care with classifying clients' spiritual and religious orientations (137). The following typologies represent general and differing levels of spiritual and religious commitment; they are not content-specific. Referenced are some common situations and approaches to consider when incorporating the spiritual and religious dimension with clients.

Clients Who Are Very Religious
Because for these clients religion/spirituality represents a large segment of their worldview and lifestyle that it makes good sense to effectively integrate spirituality into therapy (Plante 116). Generally, these clients welcome the inclusion of a religious—spiritual orientation into the treatment process. These religiously or spiritually committed clients are usually prepared to engage in therapy from the conviction of their religious beliefs and values, which can significantly influence

and impact the counseling dynamics (Kelly 137). The counselor can expect for these committed clients to be motivated to
use spiritual beliefs for insight and problem solving (Kelly
139). There are, however, those spiritual-religious clients who
are open to the spiritual dimensions without a connection to
religion or to a specific framework of religious beliefs or practices (Kelly 139). These clients have an openmindedness to
consider exploring spirituality in counseling as a therapeutic
benefit in the search for new meaning and perspectives for
growth and problem alleviation (Kelly 140).

Some highly religious-spiritual clients have what is called
"spiritual inflexibility" by Paragment. Spiritual inflexibility
occurs when clients can be unyielding, dictatorial, and con-
trolling in their beliefs, with fear at the root (qtd. in Plante
117). Highly religious clients feel that their way is the only
correct path and anyone that opposes them is misguided or a
heathen (Plante 117). "Spiritual bypassing" is another condition that could be possessed by highly religious–spiritual
clients. Spiritual bypassing, as labeled by Welwood, describes
a spiritual practice of avoidance to deal with the emotions,
needs, and other unresolved issues (qtd. in Cunningham 43).
Also classified as an imbalance or preoccupation of spirituality, or an unwillingness to face or explore psychological
issues, because the client is in bypass mode or denial because
of spiritual beliefs (Cashwell and Young 284).

Religious loyalist clients are those who follow and believe
the loyalties passed on by family, community, and society
from one generation to another. Albany describes these loyalties as part of a bundle that contains familial and ethnic
norms and practices that are cumulative and unconscious
traditions. These loyalties have many positive and negative
influences; they are intermingled and a customary part of the
culture and regulations of particular religions (qtd. in Kelly
137–38). The institutional and cultural loyalties are second-
ary to the religious loyalist's choice to consider alternatives,
although influential loyalties do not replace a person's own
autonomy (Kelly 138). Counselors need to be aware of the

significance of religious concepts and loyalties as they apply to understanding clients' culture or social behaviors with respect to making changes or adjusting to the developmental process, pathology, crisis issues, or problems clients present (Kelly 138). Because of the rigid mindsets of some highly religious clients, therapy can be arduous; often it is those challenges and interpersonal disturbances that motivate those clients to seek mental health treatment (Plante 117). Plante suggests that spiritual resources can be used to help those clients become more adaptive and flexible (117). Kelly states that counselors need to be sensitive to a client's religiosity, values, and beliefs to facilitate the therapeutic process (136).

Finally, clinicians should seek to collaborate with clergy and other religious authorities within religious traditions to help their clients grow personally and spiritually. Some religious officials are supportive of mental health professionals and issues (Plants 117). As well, Kelly suggests, for those highly religious clients who are deeply entrenched in intensive beliefs, that therapists consider the option of consultation with or referral to an empathetic clergy, pastor, or religious leader as obligatory and good clinical practice to further assist those clients (218).

Clients Who Are Not Religious
Clients who are not religious, or identified as agnostic or atheist can also profit from spiritual tools and interventions (Plante 118). Many of the interventions described in this study can certainly be suitable for the nonreligious client. There are techniques that can benefit the nonreligious client, such as rituals, social connections, and other secular experiences that are without religious—spiritual associations (Plants 119). For some clients, however, who are spiritually—religiously intolerant or indifferent to religion and spirituality, it would be inappropriate for the counselor to incorporate spiritual practices (Kelly 140). These clients' point of view should be respected, although the therapist could explore the source of their indifference or hostility. Then, without engag-

ing any spiritual-religious interventions, the therapist could determine if secular tools could meet the client's needs and improve well-being (Plante 120). Kelly proposes that counselors work to facilitate healthy outcomes supported by interventions that produce emotional and behavioral change, while omitting religion/spirituality (141).

Clients with Destructive Religious Views, Crises, and Behaviors

Mental health professionals need to be aware of clients with destructive religious views and behaviors, which can lead to destructive actions toward self or others. The therapist should deal with any matters of abuse, neglect, or other pertinent issues (Plante 127). Many of these issues carry legal implications along with mandated reporting to police and child protective agencies that breaks confidentiality (Plante 127). There are other, less-severe religious beliefs and behaviors that do not lead to serious risk factors or legal action, but bring about psychological, behavioral, and interpersonal problems or devastation among clients (Plante 127). Plante asserts that counselors dealing with the differences and conflicts over beliefs, actions, and behaviors that are damaging need to also balance and minimize hazards; while being respectful of such beliefs. Therapists must still provide a standard of care, and this is where consultation with clergy or other religious leaders may help treatment and should be considered in the best interest of the client (129).

Dark Night Journey

Dark night journey is a concept coined by St. John of the Cross, it occurs in two phases: *a night of sense*—where the person's religious and spiritual life or practices cease to bring fulfillment or a sense of connection to the divine—and a *dark night of the soul,* whereby the individual experiences a great sense of desolation and detachment, which usually results in a crisis of faith (Cashwell and Young 168). Kelly defines the dark night of sense as a phase or cycle of spiritual dryness

and abandonment in which a person is unable to pray and receive spiritual solace from God (68). The dark night is a spiritual crisis depicted as an "abyss experience," pain and suffering of the unknown, and the "cave" is about darkness (Cunningham 95). The *dark night* journey is specifically related to a loss of fellowship with God, but can precipitate a clinical depression (Cashwell and Young 168). Depression and *dark night* do share similar cognitive features of despondency, helplessness, decreased motivation, and the ruin of self-confidence (Cashwell and Young 168). In the *dark night of the soul*, the impairments are not classified, as in major depression, and a sense of humor is maintained (Kelly 86). For the counselor, the essence of the work with clients is to light candles for those who experience the dark night journey. Elkins declares, "The authentic therapist is a lit candle of being that lights the candle that has gone out in the client's soul" (185).

Spirituality of Imperfection
The spirituality of imperfection starts with the ideal that to err is human. Kurtz and Ketcham state that the beginning of spirituality is the acceptance of our being flawed and fractured and the understanding of what it means to be wounded and what it means to be whole, healed. Spirituality of imperfection initiates the notion that trying to be perfect is a cataclysmic human mistake: by coming to terms with our errors, shortcomings, mistakes, and the illusion of control, we can find the serenity we crave (2, 5). Kurtz and Ketcham define spirituality of imperfection as mainly a spirituality of "not having all the answers." A spirituality that deals with the here and now, by living humanely as well as one can and learning to live with imperfection (14, 18).

Spirituality of imperfection influences the counseling dynamics. It allows for client's spirituality to become a search for reality, for honesty, and for integrity to see and face one's self as one is: faulty, warts, and imperfect (Kurtz and Ketcham 20). It turns into a cry for help; when we seek help for what we cannot accomplish alone, we admit to our limitations and weaknesses. Spirituality is born in our acceptance and acknowledgement that we are not in control (Kurtz and Ketcham 21). Kurtz and Ketcham confirm that suffering is an inevitable part of the spirituality of imperfection. It is the first work of grace is to begin to understand that something is wrong: We are not in control and we do not have all the answers. Spirituality of imperfections embraces the dark sides, the down sides, of human experience and comprehends the experiences of imperfect beings (28). Spirituality is not therapy, although both concepts strive to "make whole:" therapy seeks what spirituality seeks, healing and wellness. The paths are divergent with different outcomes, but not in conflict (Kurtz and Ketcham 26). Counselors take the journey through the vicissitudes of life with our clients as they explore and examine their spirituality of imperfection that offers dynamic aspects to engage within the therapeutic setting, leading towards transformation and healing. Therein, counseling honors the progress of that journey, not perfection in the result. "Our wounds are often the openings into the best and most beautiful part of us."—David Richo

VII.
Epilogue

This dissertation addressed the fourteen core spiritual competencies as approved by ASERVIC and endorsed by ACA as a guide for integrating religion/spirituality into clinical practice. Competencies were developed for the competent, ethical practice of addressing spiritual and religious issues in counseling. These competencies encourage a careful examination of the six facets: worldview, self-awareness, human and spiritual development, communication, assessment, diagnosis, and treatment illustrated by the fourteen competencies. The competencies are customary instructions and directives to help mental health professionals navigate an ongoing commitment to incorporate and implement spirituality and religion into counseling.

The counseling profession is at an incredible crossroad with regard to the inclusion of spirituality and religion into the counseling dynamic. The significance of the task is clearly delineated, yet there is so much more that needs to be accomplished with ongoing training and education for appropriate implementation. Research will be crucial to establishing the impact and best practices of spirituality—religion-oriented interventions and approaches in treatment. The spiritual dimension has a component of the mysterious that can never be fully explained along with the science and the art; there is that factor of the known and the unknown. Therefore, achieving proficiency and therapeutic stability between the mystery, the science, and the art can enable mental health professionals to practice more ethically and competently, which is vital to the process and dynamics of counseling and psychotherapy.

For mental health professionals, this quest to incorporate

spirituality into counseling and psychotherapy is a continual and ongoing process of seeking more knowledge and self-examination to grow in their understanding and to increase competency in this domain Clinicians need to be aware of their own strengths and limitations with the integration of spiritual and religious dimensions. It is incumbent on counselors to have participated in a spiritual expedition and process inward for their own spiritual development. The practice of integrating spirituality into counseling should inspire counselors to address the translative and transformative aspects of meaning and purpose that deal with spiritual practices and experiences. This would honor a client's beliefs while facilitating psychospiritual growth on a level that meets clients where they are. Finally, counselors should embrace the therapeutic relevance of integrating spirituality and religion into counseling; it is an enduring commitment and, therefore intrinsic for counselors doing clinical practice. "As far as we can discern, the sole purpose of human existence is to kindle a light in the darkness of mere being."—Carl Jung

Competencies for Addressing Spiritual and Religious Issues in Counseling

Culture and Worldview
The professional counselor can describe the similarities and differences between spirituality and religion, including the basic beliefs of various spiritual systems, major world religions, agnosticism, and atheism.

The professional counselor recognizes that the client's beliefs (or absence of beliefs) about spirituality and/or religion are central to his or her worldview and can influence psychosocial functioning.

Counselor Self-Awareness
The professional counselor actively explores his or her own attitudes, beliefs, and values about spirituality and/or religion.

The professional counselor continuously evaluates the influence of his or her own spiritual and/or religious beliefs and values on the client and the counseling process.

The professional counselor can identify the limits of his or her understanding of the client's spiritual and/or religious perspective and is acquainted with religious and spiritual resources and leaders who can be avenues for consultation and to whom the counselor can refer.

Human and Spiritual Development
The professional counselor can describe and apply various models of spiritual and/or religious development and their relationship to human development.

Communication
The professional counselor responds to client communications about spirituality and/or religion with acceptance and sensitivity.

The professional counselor uses spiritual and/or religious concepts that are consistent with the client's spiritual and/or religious perspectives and are acceptable to the client.

The professional counselor can recognize spiritual and/or religious themes in client communication and is able to address these with the client when they are therapeutically relevant.

Assessment

During the intake and assessment processes, the professional counselor strives to understand a client's spiritual and/or religious perspective by gathering information from the client and/or other sources.

Diagnosis and Treatment

When making a diagnosis, the professional counselor recognizes that the client's spiritual and/or religious perspectives can a) enhance well-being; b) contribute to client problems; and/or c) exacerbate symptoms

The professional counselor sets goals with the client that are consistent with the client's spiritual and/or religious perspectives.

The professional counselor is able to a) modify therapeutic techniques to include a client's spiritual and/or religious perspectives, and b) utilize spiritual and/or religious practices as techniques when appropriate and acceptable to a client's viewpoint.

The professional counselor can therapeutically apply theory and current research supporting the inclusion of a client's spiritual and/or religious perspectives and practices.

Revised and Approved, 5/5/2009 ©ASERVIC 5/5/09
NOTE: The American Counseling Association (ACA) has now endorsed *The Spiritual Competencies*

Works Cited

American Counseling Association. *"ACA code of Ethics."* Alexandria, VA: American Counseling Association, 2005. Print

American Psychological Association. *Ethical Principles of Psychologists and Code of Conduct, 1992.* Web. 16 Oct. 2012.

American Psychiatric Association. *Diagnostic and Statistical Manual of Mental Disorders (4th ed.).* Washington, DC: American Psychiatric Association: 1994. Print.

Association for Spiritual, Ethical, and Religious Values in Counseling 2009. "Competencies for addressing Spiritual and Religious issues in counseling." *Association for Spiritual, Ethical, and Religious Values in Counseling, 2009.* Web. 16 Oct 2012.

Bandura, Albert (Therapy Quotes). "By sticking it out through tough times, people emerge from adversity with a stronger sense of efficacy" 8 April 2013. Tweet.

Blando, John A. "Spirituality, Religion, and Counseling." *Counseling and Human_Development* 39.2 (2006): 1-14. Web. 16 Jan. 2013.

Burke, Mary Thomas, and Judith G. Miranti. *Counseling the Spiritual Dimension.* Alexandria: American Counseling Association. 1995. Print.

Cashwell, Craig S., and J. Scott Young, eds. *Integrating Spirituality and Religion into Counseling: A Guide to Competent Practice.* Alexandria: American Counseling Association. 2011. Print.

Chandler, Cynthia K., Janice Miner Holden, and Cheryl A. Kolander. "Counseling for Spiritual Wellness: Theory and Practice." *Journal of Counseling & Development* 71 Nov./Dec. (1992): 168-175. Print.

Clark, M. Carolyn, and Rosemary S. Caffarella, eds. "Update on Adult Development Theory: New Ways of Thinking about the Life Course." *New Directions for Adult and Continuing Education* 84 Winter (1999): 1-106. Print.

Corey, Gerald. "Integrating Spirituality in Counseling Practice". *Vistas Online* Article 25 (2006): 117-119. Web. 16 Oct 2012.

Council for Accreditation of Counseling and Related Educational Programs. 2009. *"Standards" Council for Accreditation of Counseling and Related Educational Programs.* Web. 8 April 2013. < http://www.cacrep.org/doc/2009%20 Standards%20with%20cover.pdf>.

Cunningham, Maddy. *Integrating Spirituality in Clinical Social Work Practice: Walking the Labyrinth.* Boston: Pearson Education, 2012. Print.

Elkins, David. *Beyond religion.* Wheaton, IL: Quest Books, 1998. Print

Ellison, Craig W. and Joel Smith. "Toward an Integrative Measure of Health and Well-Being." *Journal of Psychology and Theology.* 19.1 (1991): 35-48. Print.

Fukuyama, Mary A., and Todd D. Sevig. *Integrating Spirituality into Multicultural Counseling.* Thousand Oaks, CA: Sage, 1999. Print.

Gellman, Mari, and Thomas Hartman. *Religion for Dummies.* New York: Wiley, 2002. Print.

Gross, Stanley J. "The Holistic Movement." *The Personal and Guidance Journal* 59 (1980): 96-100. Print.

Grimm, Donald W. "Therapist Spiritual and Religious Values in Psychotherapy." *Counseling and Values* 38 April (1994): 154-64. Print.

Harper, Frederick D. and John McFadden. eds. *Culture and Counseling: New Approaches.* Boston: Pearson Education, 2003. Print.

Hinterkopf, Elfie. *Integrating Spirituality in Counseling: A Manual for Using the Experiential Focusing Method.* Alexandria: American Counseling Association, 1998.

Print.

Hughes, Betty. "The Creative Use of Spirituality to Enhance Pychotherapy". *Counseling Outfitters*. Web. 16 Oct 2012. <http://counselingoutfitters.com/vistas/vistas11/article_101.pdf>

Ingersoll R. Elliot. "Spirituality, Religion, and Counseling: Dimensions and Relationship." *Counseling and Values* January 38 (1994): 99-111. Print.

Jowett, Benjamin. *The Dialogues of Plato.* New York: Random House, 1937. Print.

Jongsma, Arthur, E., Jr., L. Mark Peterson, and Timothy J. Bruce. eds. *The Complete Adult Psychotherapy Treatment Planner*, 4th ed. Hoboken: Wiley, 2006. Print.

Kelly, Eugene W. *Spirituality and Religion in Counseling and Psychotherapy: Diversity in Theory and Practice*. Alexandria: American Counseling Association. 1995. Print.

Kurtz, Ernest, and Katherine Ketcham. *The Spirituality of Imperfection: Storytelling and the Search for Meaning*. New York: Bantam Books, 1992. Print.

Lish, R. Allen. "Religious/Spiritual Issues in the Counseling Room: What Pastors Knew all along." *New Hope Professional Psychological Services*. Web. 5 Sept 2012. <http://www.newhopepps.org/docs/Religious%20and%20Spiritual%20Issues%20in%20Counseling%20-%20for%20pas.pdf>

Mattson, Donald L. "Religious Counseling: To Be Used, Not Feared." *Counseling and Values* 38 Apr. (1994): 187-192. Print.

Meier, Augustine, Thomas St James O' Connor, and Peter L. Vankatwky. eds. *Spirituality and health: Multidisciplinary Explorations*. Ontario: Wilfrid Laurier University 2005. Print.

Meyers, Jane E. "Wellness Throughout the Life Span." *Guidepost*. 12 (1990) 11-22. Print.

Moore, Thomas. *Care of the Soul: A Guide for Cultivating*

Depth and Sacredness in Everyday Life. New York: Harper-Perennial, 1992. Print.

Plante, Thomas G. *Spiritual Practices in Psychotherapy: Thirteen Tools for Enhancing Psychological Health.* Washington: American Psychological Association, 2009. Print.

Richards, P. Scott and Allen E Bergin. *A Spiritual Strategy for Counseling and Psychotherapy,* 2nd ed. Washington: American Psychological Association. 2005 Print.

Sperry, Len. *Spirituality in Clinical Practice: Incorporating the Spiritual Dimension in Psychotherapy and Counseling.* Ann Arbor: Brunner-Routledge, 2001. Print.

Steen, Rheta LeAnne, Dennis Engels, and W. Thweatt, "Ethical aspects of Spirituality in Counseling" *Counseling in Values* 50.2 (2006): 108-118.Web. 13 Nov. 2012.

Sutton, Amy L. *Complementary and Alternative Medicine Source Book.* 4th ed. (Health reference series). Detroit: Omnigraphics, 2010. Print.

Uomoto, Jay D. "Psychotherapy as Soul Care" *Gestalt! Editorial.*(1997). Web. 26 Jan. 2013.

Zinn, Lorraine M. Spirituality in Adult Education. *Adult Learning* 8 (1997): 5-6, 26-30. Print.

Addendum: Counselor's Quick Pick
Suggested Reading
Quotes
Inspirational bible scriptures
Closing Prayer

Suggested Reading List

Your Soul's Plan Discovering the Real Meaning of the Life You Planned Before You Were Born by Robert Schwartz.

Rent Two Films and Let's Talk in the Morning Using Popular Movies in Psychotherapy by John W. Hesley & Jan G. Hesley.

Who moved my Cheese? by Spencer Johnson

There's a Spiritual Solution to Every Problem by Dr. Wayne W. Dyer

Manifest Your Destiny: The Nine Spiritual Principles for Getting Everything You Want by Dr. Wayne W. Dyer

The Four Agreements: A Practical Guide to Personal Freedom (A Toltec Wisdom Book) Don Miguel Ruiz

The Steven Spiritual Laws of Success: A Practical Guide to the Fulfillment of Your Dreams by Deepak Chopra

Spiritual Solutions: Answers to Life's Greatest Challenges by Deepak Chopra

20 (Surprisingly Simple) RULES and TOOLS for a GREAT DAY by Dr. Steve Stephens

The Highly Sensitive Person by Elaine N. Aron, Ph.D

Secret to Serenity Transforming from Sexual Abuse to Spiritual healing by Chrysty Sturdivant and Nina Rios-Doria.

Quick Scripture Reference For Counseling Third Edition by John G. Kruisas

The Biblical Basis of Christian Counseling for People Helpers by Gary R. Collins, Ph.D.

THE FEELING GOOD HANDBOOK revised by David D. Burns, M.D.

Purpose Driven Life by Rick Warren

Your Best Life Now by Joel Osteen

One Day My Soul just Opened Up by Iyanla Vanzant

Peace from Broken Pieces: How to Get Through What You're Going Through by Iyanla Vanzant.

The Road Less Traveled by M Scott Peck

Think and Grow Rich by Napoleon Hill

Feel the Fear and Do it Anyway by Susan Jeffers

A New Earth: Awakening to Your Life's Purpose by Eckhart Tolle

Conversations with God: An Uncommon Dialogue, Book 1 by Neale Donald Walsch

Don't Sweat the Small Stuff… and it all small stuff by Richard Carlson, PH.D

Awaken the Giant Within by Anthony Robbins

The Power of Positive Thinking by Norman Vincent Peale

How to Win Friends and Influence People by Dale Carnegie

The Alchemist by Paulo Coelho

Achieve Anything in Just One Year: Be Inspired Daily to Live Your Dreams and Accomplish Your Goals Paperback by Jason Harvey

Ask and it is Given: Learning to Manifest Your Desires by Esther and Jerry Hicks

Battlefield of the Mind: Winning the Battle in Your Mind by Joyce Meyers

A Return to Love by Marianne Williamson

Life without limits: Inspiration for a Ridiculously Good Life by Nick Vujicic

Quotes for Mental Health Therapy

"We are not human beings having a spiritual experience. We are spiritual beings having a human experience."
                                    - Pierre Teilhard de Chardin

"You cannot solve a problem from the same consciousness that created it. You must learn to see the world anew."
                                    – Albert Einstein

"Love the moment. Flowers grow out of dark moments. Therefore, each moment is vital. It affects the whole. Life is a succession of such moments and to live each, is to succeed."
                                    –Sister Mary Corita

"Depression is the inability to construct a future."
                                    - Rollo May

"When I is replaced by WE, even illness becomes wellness."
                                    – unknown

"I am not what happened to me, I am what I choose to become."
                                    – Carl Jung

"What we see changes what we know. What we know changes what we see."
                                    —Jean Piaget

"People have a fundamental need for transformation. We are wired for growth and healing."
                                    – Diana Fosha

"Our deepest fear is not that we are inadequate. Our deepest fear is that we are powerful beyond measure. It is our

light, not our darkness that most frightens us. We ask ourselves, Who am I to be brilliant, gorgeous, talented, fabulous? Actually, who are you not to be?"
- Marianne Williamson, A Return to Love: Reflections on the Principles of "A course in Miracles."

"Life isn't about waiting for the storm to pass; it's about learning to dance in the rain."
– Vivian Greene

"Let us not look back in anger or forward in fear, but around in awareness."
- James Thurber

"A life unexamined is not worth living"
– Socrates

"Our wounds are often the openings into the best and most beautiful part of us."
- David Richo

"The only person who cannot be helped is that person who blames others."
– Carl Jung

"The curious paradox is that when I accept myself just as I am, then I can change."
–Carl Jung

"I'm not perfect...but I'm enough."
–Carl Rogers

"We must be broken into life."
–Charles E. Raven

"We create ourselves by our choices."
–Kierkegaard

"Strive for progression not perfection."
　　　　　　　　　　　　　　　　　—Unknown

"Be kind, for everyone you meet is fighting a harder battle."
　　　　　　　　　　　　　　　　　　　　—Plato

"We are products of our past, but we don't have to be prisoners of it."
　　*—Rick Warren, The Purpose Driven Life: What on Earth
　　　　　　　　　　　　　　　Am I here for?"*

"We grow and heal when we take every event and find its blessing.
　　　　　　　　　—Debbie Ford, Spiritual Divorce"

"Bumps are the things we climb on."
　　　　　　　　　　　　　　—Warren Wiersbe

"There are only two ways to live your life. One is as though nothing is a miracle the other is as though everything is a miracle."
　　　　　　　　　　　　　　　　—Albert Einstein

"There is only one corner of the universe that you can be certain of improving and that's your own self."
　　　　　　　　　　　　　　　　—Aldous Huxley

"You cannot have a positive life and a negative mind."
　　　　　　　　　　　　　　　　—Joyce Meyers

"If you only do what is easy, you will always remain weak."
　　　　　　　　　　　　　　　　—Joyce Meyers

"Our habits, good or bad, are something we can control."
　　　　　　　　　　　　　—Dr. E.J. Stieglitz

"God put rainbows in the clouds so that each of us- in the dreariest and most dreaded moments-can see a possibility of hope."

—*Maya Angelou*

"There is no greater agony than bearing an untold story inside you."

—*Maya Angelou*

"I can be changed by what happens to me. But I refuse to be reduced by it."

—*Maya Angelou*

"It is to be prayed that the mind be sound in a sound body."
—*Juvenal*

23 Inspirational Bible Verses for clinicians and clients

International Standard Version (ISV)   Proverbs 12:15
The lifestyle of the fool is right in his own opinion, but wise is the man who listens to advice.

English Standard Version (ESV)   Proverbs 13:20
Whoever heeds life-giving correction will be at home among the wise.

English Standard Version (ESV)   Proverbs 19:20
Listen to advice and accept instruction, that you may gain wisdom in the future.

English Standard Version (ESV)   Proverbs 11:14
Where there is no guidance, a people falls, but in an abundance of counselors there is safety.

World English Bible (WEB)   Proverbs 15:22
Where there is no counsel, plans fail; but in a multitude of counselors they are established.

King James Version (KJV)   Proverbs 3:5
Trust in the LORD with all your heart and lean not on your own understanding.

King James Version (KJV)   2 Timothy 1:7
For God hath not given us the spirit of fear; but of power, and of love, and of a sound mind.

New International Version (NIV)   James 1:5
If any of you lacks wisdom, you should ask God, who gives generously to all without finding fault, and it will be given to you.

New International Version (NIV)   Ecclesiastes 8:6
For there is a proper time and procedure for every matter, though a person may be weighed down by misery.

King James Version (KJV)   Ecclesiastes 3:1,4
To every *thing* there is a season, and a time to every purpose under the heaven...A time to weep, and a time to laugh; a time to mourn, and a time to dance;

English Standard Version (ESV)   1 Peter 5:7
7 casting all your anxieties on him, because he cares for you.

King James Version (KJV)   Proverbs 46:10
Be still, and know that I *AM GOD*

English Standard Version (ESV)   Psalm 119:105
Your word is a lamp to my feet and a light to my path.

English Standard Version (ESV)   Psalm 119:130
The unfolding of your words gives light; it imparts understanding to the simple.

New International Version (NIV)   Matthew 6:22
The eye is the lamp of the body. If your eyes are healthy, your whole body will be full of light.

King James Version (KJV)   Matthew 5:16
Let your light so shine before men, that they may see your good works, and glorify your Father which is in heaven.

World English Bible (WEB)   Psalm 42:5
Why are you in despair, my soul? Why are you disturbed within me? Hope in God! For I shall still praise him for the saving help of his presence.

International Standard Version (ISV)   Job 33:28
He has redeemed my soul from going down into the Pit, and my life will see the light.

World English Bible (WEB)   Philippians 4:8-9
8 Finally, brothers, whatever things are true, whatever things are honorable, whatever things are just, whatever things are pure, whatever things are lovely, whatever things are of good report; if there is any virtue, and if there is any praise, think about these things. **9** The things which you learned, received, heard, and saw in me: do these things, and the God of peace will be with you.

King James Version (KJV)   Proverbs 15:13
A merry heart maketh a cheerful countenance: but by sorrow of the heart the spirit is broken.

New International Version (NIV)   Psalm 23:1-4
1 The LORD is my shepherd, I lack nothing. **2** He makes me lie down in green pastures, he leads me beside quiet waters, **3** he refreshes my soul. He guides me along the right paths for his name's sake. **4** Even though I walk through the darkest valley,[a] I will fear no evil, for you are with me; your rod and your staff, they comfort me.

New International Version (NIV)   Romans 12:12
Be joyful in hope, patient in affliction, faithful in prayer.

New International Version (NIV)   Proverbs 20:5
The purposes of a person's heart are deep waters, but one who has insights draws them out.

Closing Prayer

The Serenity Prayer

God grant me the serenity
to accept the things I cannot change;
courage to change the things I can;
and wisdom to know the difference.

Living one day at a time;
enjoying one moment at a time;
accepting hardships as the pathway to peace;
taking, as He did, this sinful world
as it is, not as I would have it;
trusting that He will make all things right
if I surrender to His Will;
that I may be reasonably happy in this life
and supremely happy with Him
forever in the next.
Amen.

—Reinhold Niebuhr

CPSIA information can be obtained
at www.ICGtesting.com
Printed in the USA
LVHW080458150421
684598LV00019B/1004

9 781480 917507